JAMERICAN POETRY

PAULETTE LEWIS

authorHOUSE®

AuthorHouse™
1663 Liberty Drive
Bloomington, IN 47403
www.authorhouse.com
Phone: 1 (800) 839-8640

Published by AuthorHouse 04/07/2016

ISBN: 978-1-5246-0259-8 (sc)
ISBN: 978-1-5246-0258-1 (e)

Print information available on the last page.

This book is printed on acid-free paper.

CONTENTS

TWO COUNTRY DIAMOND.

Two country Diamond.
One country will hold the
Setting.
The other country will have
Access to the mold.
One is hot hot hot but fun
The other is freezer cold and
Bold.
One will go searching until
they find gold.
The other will stand by with no
problem at all.
Two Countries my place, my home
Safety is the glue for attributes.
Love for all is the Avenue.
Two beautiful hearts made of gold.
Jamaica, America Paradise on the
Throne.

EVERYDAY IS A HOLIDAY

Everyday is a holiday
Celebrate every moment
Enter your mindset with your
Favorite music.
Turn this poem into a song..
Marinade your thoughts and
take it along.
Pack all your passions
That will be your need
Gather all your productive seed.
Spend time exploring with your
smile intact.
Help to see the beauty in your freedom
clutch. Welcome mankind with an open arm.
Everyday is a Holiday and your'e a Charm.
Vacation is every moment well spent with the
ones you love.
Never ending, filled with surprises.

I WOKE UP TO NATURE

I woke up to nature banging on
my door.
Thunder and Lightening sounding
off galore.
With my eyes barely open, I still could say
Thank you Lord for this showers of
Blessings. Rainy day.
The wind then send the Trees swaying.
Raindrops draw me outside to deliver this
message.
Applying my creativity for this finishing touch
Glossy finish just for your Art.
Nature has a special place in my heart.
I remember the day I survived Hurricane
Gilbert and Hurricane Sandy.
Two Countries not too far apart.
I woke up to Nature, two times over.
One hand will always help the other.
Survive and appreciate Nature.
Always find cover for shelter.

THE BEAUTY WE SHARE

The beauty we share, will last
forever.
The memories sleeps in our Hearts
Today the Tree of life gets wiser
Live to learn and to prosper better.
The beauty we share will be a door to
uplift others.
Be Positive with no Negative glue.
Let your gift guide you to a world
beyond your view.
Shine your light in the darkness
Send your love to unlock the clue.
Solve your dream in one simple step.
The beauty we share will always be
with you. First impression so True.

WITHIN THE SPACE

Within the space of every moment
you will find peace.
In the Calm before every minute
you will find Avenue Breeze
True happiness awaits you.
Step in your Zone. Fine a comfort
to welcome your Soul home.
Humble is knocking at your door
Open with a grateful heart.
Within the space you will find
comfort, and a monitor to guide
you along.
Safety is your friend, follow the
light that forever lives on in you.
Seek more time to help others.
Within the space.
Uplift the one that will need a pacemaker.

HONOR THY GOD.

Honor thy God
Remove yourself from every
stressful situation.
Hand every burden at his feet.
Hustle and bustle is no longer a
factor.
Come on let's read a Chapter.
Honor thy God he's ahead of
your dreams.
Inside your soul he will send you
a psalms.
Read and make your home in his
arms. Greater is his words for you.
Respect travel on this journey.
Honor thy God and recognize his name.

DRESS TO IMPRESS ONE

Dress to impress
Our heavenly father
already know how we
feel.
He gave us confidence
to use and butter appeal.
He compliment our hearts
to make bread.
With food on our table and
Roof over our heads.
Dress is the base to carry our
presence.
Feel good then welcome yourself.
Dress to impress.
You're beautiful.
Compliment others.
Nice Tie.
Hi and bye.

CONTINUE GIVING

Continue giving
Allow Brotherly love
and Sisterly love to abide
in you.
Share in every aspect of
life. You can never give
too much away.
Your blessing will be for
others to enjoy too.
Continue giving my dear
Jesus is always at your
front door to bless you.
Good health to you.
Every gift you give
clears your heart to give
more.
Continue giving this is a
chore.
Well, hello how do you do?

FROM MY TENT

From my Tent
I can smell the Roses.
From my Tent I can see
no blue.
From my Tent I erase all
troubles, Survival is my
Avenue.
Faith food and Shelter is
my daily bread to give.
My positive outlook is hanging
over my head. Everyday is a
Gratitude shoulder to give me
a hug. Family and friends are
close by.
Writing is my passion to live.
From my Tent I can see the ocean.
Far away is my favorite Bird.
Deeper in the Distant, I Pray to see
the top of my Palm Tree.
Blowing in the wind.
From my Tent, I will welcome everyone.
To come home.

PERFECT TEN

Perfect ten, what perfect ten
No one is perfect so I will tell you
when. Score your first goal for your
Team then soccer it over to me.
I will make a Record Base to add
your perfect ten.
Perfect Ten will be your new score
Be the body of your game, then
everyone will feel the same.
Walk with all your training in hand.
Coach your way to help others.
No one is perfect, so you can tell me
when.
Balance is needed to feel like a perfecta.
Smile and give me a hug. Welcome
good Sportsmanship.
Because no one is perfect.

WALL OF LOVE

This is the Wall of Love for you
When your mood flips
on the downside.
Focus on the wall of love.
Faith Family and Friends
will set things in motion
This is so true, not Brew.
Detox from any negative energy
Replace it with some positive
vibes, a new you.
Enjoy the ambiance that awaits
you. Calm tide.
Humble beginnings, welcome
your smile.
Your family is waiting outside.
What a surprise.
On the Wall of love.
A new me, a new you.
The Nation wall of love.
Forever bonded.

NAKED AND AFRAID

Naked and afraid
Find a leaf to cover yourself.
Read this poem with a grain of Salt.
Smile on the walls of every open space
Give back to the safety side of your face
Naked and afraid,why am I drifting to the
left side. Stroke me some sense to await
my pride.
This journey will be filled with laughter
Laugh anyway even if it gets harder.
Control your temperature, I need mind
to cross over.
Bridge me a game of Bingo.
Every gifted soul was born naked.
Be not afraid. Anyway you see it
Will be okay. Make me a naked poetry dress.
This is a test, the naked truth, is yours to keep.
Tell everyone anyway enjoy the spree.

FROM MY HEARTS TO YOURS

From my heart to yours
Sending this note with the highest degree
Feeling hot yet you could be feeling free
From my Heart, I will send my energy tease.
Be that suspense clue to wrap around my knees.
Breathe in deeply for fresh air, oh what a relief.
Survive in the moment of despair, be brief .
Revive me from a dark place of love
The one you trust just trusted the past more
From a heart filled with pain again.
Send me some happy moments to ring in the
positive tune be strong.
From my heart to yours. Thanks for being a
friend.
The beginning and never the end.

DEEP IN THE WILDERNESS

Deep in the Wilderness
Imaging if you have Palm Trees.
Travel with your water Bucket to
Quench your thirst.
Safety net is your Bible Verses.
Use less energy and more common
senses.
Focus is your happy tool
The Sun is actually your distant friend.
The Moon is in your circle,
The Stars is yours to renew.
Monitor your Vital in the mid stream of
every breath. Survival is now a scheme.
Food is not very important, fluid is the main
source. Be aware of your surroundings
Nature will give you a call. Enjoy the rain
Enjoy the meaningful messengers
The Birds will sing you a song that will be
your clue to find your way out.
Deep in the Wilderness, You will find me.
Open your eyes, I brought you Chicken Soup.
Your Guiding Angels knows where to find you.
Wake up my dear, this is a dream.
I am beside you.

I FOUND LOVE

Love was looking for me on the wrong Avenue
My Heart was stationary, yet my soul was drifting
away.
My Body was at a standstill studying the Stony Hill
My love took a turn on a Valley Road instead.
Standing there was my Daily Bread.
Gratitude was my song to sing. No good deed will
go unanswered in this poem.
I found true love with the one, that believes in himself.
Granted to me was more freedom.
With Trust holding our hands.
I found peaceful love with you
You are a gentleman.

BEAUTIFUL RAINBOW.

Beautiful Rainbow
Beautiful Hearts.
Every color in the world makes up
The Rainbow, jump start.
Enjoy every moment this time is yours
to grasp.
Beautiful Rainbow let me carry your joy at last.
Gather your surprise kit and give them away.
More beautiful Rainbow Art will come again
to stay.
Beautiful Rainbow, my dear, make a wish
Everyone will carry your blessing someday.
In the form of a Beautiful Rainbow.
A gift Just for you.
To carry me through.

THE OCEAN KNOWS MY NAME

The Ocean knows my name
My dreams are in the middle
of mid stream.
The Sun open my eyes to
Stop tears, to redeem.
I radiates in the arms of my
Jehovah's love
The Ocean knows my name
He call me friend,always at
hand to help along the way
Long walk with my dear one
kicking up sand.
Waiting for the first Bird to sing
me a song.
The Ocean knows my name
It's a Brand at hand.
Waiting to be discovered
All over again.

PROTECT YOURSELF

Protect yourself
Pull over your safety
Blanket.
Request enough positive
groove as lancet.
Massage in a safety net
Move in the direction of
Happiness.
Put on the charm when you
come over.
Protect yourself with your
Wisdom maneuver.
Love is a healthy Apple
You can only eat so much.
Swing from this poem like
it was a Chandelier.
Be safe and protect yourself
with true love.
Wrap things up on your
Birthday.
Smile and say hurrah.
Protecting is fun and easy.
Come on, tease me.
With your Strawberry.

YES TO OUR REUNION

I can't wait to see you again
Spectacular memories from
my childhood friend.
Silly and Naive was our chapter
Trusting everyone was our behavior.
Listening to our parents was on a
guessing factor.
No one can dress better than us.
Beautiful is our happy stream not
disgust.
Enjoying Nature was all over
Very little money,yet we could afford
Spectacular.
Using the Moon as a Base, Counting
the Stars for a tease, Falling asleep
under a Tree.
Hoping someday a handsome hunk
would marry me.
Time to go home,at the Rise of the Sun.
Yes to our reunion, this fun replay all
over again.
Welcome to my childhood friend.

MY VEGETABLE GARDEN

Could I sleep in my Vegetable Garden
Does my weight wraps up in these green
leaves.
Should I water then flourish with manure
For a clean sweep.
Should I build a house with no front door
So you could visit and eat. I never feel like
leaving my garden in this heat.
Pulling my mind around the tangled weed
Removing it away from my Collard greens.
My Vegetable is my new Retreat.
It detoxes my mind body and Soul then I feel
relieved.
My Vegetable Garden is a new start
To jump start my heart. V8 out of my tomatoes
Large Melons to compliment my joy.
A Vegetable Garden will send your thoughts
beyond border.
Just to invite everyone over to eat Jalapeno Peppers.

WOMAN OF STEEL

Woman of steel is the mother in
every household.
Keeping the Family together
with the snap of a finger.
Sending out orders to follow.
Loving the first born more
But will always deny it.
Spoiling the last child which they
call the wash belly, so quit.
Different Culture, same love going
around for their children background.
Woman of Steel knows your pain
Every Pressure is console by a mothers
Vein.
Woman of steel is in every culture
Forever loved by their family.
Forever.
Mother.

GIVE ENERGY TO THE WEAK

Give Energy to the weak
Boost them with some energy relief.
Uplift with your tender slide.
Humble and peace will be by your side.
Safety is not far away, give a helping
hand to the stray.
Find a home in your Heart to share
this day, when you give energy to
the weak, Mayday.
Prosper with the new energy in you.
Gratitude will go around in circle.
Next time it could be you.
In the middle of an Emergency.
Know exactly what to do.
Thirty compressions to two.
Survive on this avenue.

WILL YOU FIND TIME FOR ME

Will you find time for me
Are you still looking for
your schedule, free.
Will you find time for me
in your world tonight.
Will you find time for me
just to take a bite.
Well could we call this an
innocent fight
Fried Chicken delight.
Will you find time for me in
your spare time.
Or do I need to spare my time
in a reserve mode, Crude
Will you find time for your love.
Easy pickings from our family
Tree.
Will you find time for me.
Fun mixed with quality time.

COMMUNITY LOVE

Community Love
Send in the Flowers and
Spring some community
love on my Lawn.
I will return the favor in the
afternoon.
Send in the positive minds
with some Volunteer mood
Community love is the name
of this Avenue.
Theme is to help the elders
Console the homeless to a
Humble behavior.
A helping hand is all over
The Community love is
Forever.
One hand welcome your brother.
The other will uplift my sister.
Real Community Love.
Forever.

PRAY UNTIL YOU ARE FULFILLED

Pray in the quiet of a pen drop
Pray when you hear the word
Stop.
Pray because sometimes,that
all we got.
Pray for a peace of mind.
Pray in the beginning of a turmoil.
Pray when everything is going great
Pray when you have to give and take.
Pray in the drop of a hat
Pray when the dog chases the cat.
Pray in this wicked world
Where prayer is the best medicine.
Everyday treatment,for good health.
Pray for me, and I will pray for you
Both Prayer will be strong enough to
carry us through.
Let us pray.
Amen.

TRAVEL IN SILENCE

Travel in silence my dear
Meditate on life journey
Travel in silence,close your
eyes and remove your burden
Travel in silence without moving
a muscle. No baggage will be
stored in the upper compartment
Just the taste of your favorite mint
endurement.
Travel in silence a peaceful Agent
just pass by.
Meditate deeper he could be the
modern fly.
Wake up to the Sea filled with majestic
mood.
Travel in silence it's a groove.

WHEN MY FAITH CALLS ME HOME

When my Faith calls me home
Rejoice in your space of comfort
Share the good times we cherished
Gather all the pieces and heal the
broken hearts.
Forever our Faith family and friends
will join a togetherness.
When my Faith calls me home
Rejoice in the Lord, and bless your
Soul.
When my Faith call me home
No more pain to go around.
Just a missing piece of the puzzle
Refreshing your Love to carry on.
When my Faith call me home.
You will always remember me.
In that beautiful, beautiful garden.

THIS HOLY DAY

Putting trials and tribulation aside
Let's celebrate this Holy day.
Fasting in a world that is filled with
Sin.
Let's all find a special time to Pray.
This Holy day will be your moment
To confess all your sins.
Leaving no room for the Devil to come
in. Holy,Holy,Holy rest in the space within
your heart
Relax in your home for a Holy Cross.
Oh how I love this Holy day to pray.
Then set my mind at ease.

MERRY CHRISTMAS

Merry Christmas to you
May all your dreams come
Through.
Oh how happy I am to see you.
and you, and you.
Jesus was born on this beautiful day
So why should we stay away.
Celebration is in circulation
Christmas Carols vibration.
Baby Jesus oh what a blessing.
Heavenly father smiles from Heaven
Earthly love from everyone.
Merry Christmas
Merry Christmas
Spectacular moment is the true love
from Jesus.
Merry Christmas.
One child lived on.

DEEP IN THE DESSERT

Deep in the Dessert
With no plan of my own
Hydrated is my Brain
Putting my thinking cap on
Showing gratitude to one
Praying for a discovery channel
Hoping for another Scenery Panel
Deep in the Dessert, safety is my
pillowcase.
Focus were my eyes on the Crow.
Deep in the Dessert, Jesus is still
my best friend.
In his arm, I will lay my head.
Deep in the Dessert, I still find peace.
Peace with Nature.

CHOSEN ANGEL

My focus was always on
Feeding the poor.
I travel the world and praises
the Lord.
My journey was filled with turmoil
and pain.
Yet my goal was never to cast down
blame or shame.
My hope was never to be alone
My heart was filled with my family gone.
Don't cry for me no more my friend.
I made it on the other side through the front door.
In my last Agonal moment I was able to
take a deep breath and ask God for
forgiveness.
He then call my name Zackery Tims.
You're now safe under my wings.
Only good memories will be remembered.
Blessings to your sisters and brothers.
Welcome home my chosen Angel.
I named you Zackery Tims.

FARMERS CHILD

Yes I am a Farmers Child
Sends the rich Soil my way.
Love the Nature Cherries
Earthly things send me some
strawberries and blueberries
Lettuce and Tomatoes I will
carry in my basket.
Share with everyone that would
take it, or bake it.
Farmers child store some away
for Mr rainy day.
My eyes sparkle, because I am a
Farmers child.
Nature Wild.

PAUSE FOR A MOMENT

Reflect on the good times.
Block the bad brain attack
of failure within.
Pause for a moment, now
it comes back.
Rewind and reach for the
Positive a mode.
Play your moment in a passionate
cloud
Spread your wings and your mind
will work for you.
In this moment of time.
The sky is still blue.
Relax I am here with you.
Just press pause for a moment.

WE WILL FACE CHALLENGES

We will face challenges
We will face shame
We will face life with a
number to gain
We will ask questions
Yet to wait for an answer
would be in vain.
So we learn to shuffle our
way around.
We learn to face things alone
We will face challenges
In every journey.
Wrap your brain around it and
make it your friend.
Feed on positive vibes until the
end my friend.
Winning is easy, you were never
alone, in all your many challenges
Jesus was with you.

JAMAICAN POLITICS

Caos is everywhere
Fear sets in to win.
Truth is mixed in with
suspense to spice things up.
Faith is no longer in front of you.
It's now in the middle with it's
mouth wide open. You have to
be kidding.
The one that will survive will master
maneuvering.
Extra bonus when you order groceries
Something strange between the flour and
the sugar. Money talks my fellowmen
Vote for the one that give you bread.
Jamaican Politics has no rules.
Fun when you think about the leaders
in charge. Caos in the poor man
child head. Please Lord come over
I want to live in America.
Jamaican Politics will play the same tune forever.

NO ONE IS EXEMPT FROM MY LOVE

No one is exempt from my love
You're in my only will
No one is exempt from my love.
Good or bad I love you still.
Straighten up, let go of your guilt
Someday you could save the world
with your Quilt.
Magnificent is my love for you.
Use it to carry you through
life journey will be survived by a few.
Nothing is exempt from my love.
Not even the turtle Dove.

AMERICAN POLITICS.

American Politics is like having a
no Disaster Plan.
Nothing is off limit, everyone is
exposed to be contaminated.
CNN push the plug all the way
to the bank. Excessive work of the
Negative force.
The truth went on Vacation to Jamaica
Leaving politics to fend for itself.
Believe in whatever, you're correct.
Take notes of what makes no sense.
Smile when you see that you could
be smarter than the American President.
A poor man child faces more challenges.
That's the positive that will be strong enough
to run the Nation.
American Politics need a mandatory inservice.
Judge not, or else you will be wide open to be
Judged.
Spread the country with a safety net.
Prayer first.
Meditation immediately after.

ADVOCATE FOR THE POOR

Advocate for the poor will have
to put on a protective gear.
Safety first in every Career.
Boost up security know the right
gear.
Whenever abuse shows it's head
say beware.
Stand firm in your wilderness hold
your gait.
You're his voice, please don't be late.
Firmly your prayer will be answered.
Always bless by God.
Advocate for the poor, now please
open the door, and welcome all.

EXTRAORDINARY ONE

The things that are beyond the ordinary
The things that seems beyond your reach
Yet you find Able to hand it to you.
In the palm of your hand, you wear the
golden shoe on your feet.
Far away in the distance, I could see you.
Searching the Ocean for a new Avenue.
Extraordinary one, feels your pain.
Yet in your world you will have a lot to gain.
Finding happiness as your true friend.
Extraordinary one.

VOLUNTEER

Volunteering as an EMT
was easy.
I love to help people.
Survival is always an
Emergency gate.
So a Volunteer has lots
of love in their hearts.
Look,listen,feel then call
for help.
Safety to use as a bed rest.
Cover all basics in documenting
Volunteers should have wings.
Build Fountains,build mountains
and Bridges.
Hats off to all Volunteer Teams.

QUEEN OF POETRY

The queen of poetry has Pizzazz
Shows confidence like it was in a
conference.
Walk with no particular attitude
So you can't make sense.
The Queen of poetry
Smile for the Camera
Work the run way with no order.
Sending traffic on a journey.
Marching the Band with from a
distance.
Queen of Poetry is extraordinary.
Not out here to please everybody.
Just here to splash love all over the
screen.
For everyone to read.

KNOW YOUR ASSIGNMENT

Collect your thoughts
Focus on the main
requirement needed
to complete your course..
Gather main facts to balance
your task.
Reach for the highest mindset
Use it to be your secret.
Blend in with your assignment
One unity to win a challenge.
Smile at the end of the race
Knowing is the first base.
Your assignment is now complete.
With you outside a box.

BIRTHDAY NEWS

Today is someones birthday
Yesterday was someones birthday
Tomorrow will be someone birthday.
Birthday news is still on their way
Prepare the cake for a surprise anyway.
Send in the extra bonus find your gift.
Prepare to give Birthday news a lift.
Happy Birthday is looking for you.
Outside is your new Avenue
Shout from the open space that boost
your heart Rate.
Birthday News is now your treat.
Enjoy with lots to eat.
Smile, let me tickle your feet.
Birthday News have us on Tv.
Celebrating with the rest of the world.

BY YOUR BEDSIDE

I am in your space for a moment
Enjoy this special present .
Gifted to you is my helping hand
Uplifting in this difficult time spand.
Praying for a speedy recovery
Praying is the strongest medicine.
Peaceful is your soul.
I am in your space just for awhile.
Sharing love by your bedside.
Forever will abide.

NO MAN SHOULD PERISH

Mistakes will be made
Truth will be told.
Forever we will learn and grow.
Finding deep peace is far and in
between.
Every task is a test, but no man
should perish, for the untold.
Find a common ground and plant
Success Bold.
Some people will be happier working
for less.
Feed the poor regardless.
In every field, no man should perish.
This is your test.

MY HEART WELCOME YOU

My Heart welcomes you home.
My Soul crippled in your arms.
Feeling like a prodigal child.
No need to press the alarm.
Get all your burden and lay them
aside.
Be my shoulder to lean on for awhile.
My Heart welcomes you home.
Around the bend you will find forgiveness.
Use it to comfort your soul.
Be brave,be bold because
My Heart welcomes you home.

GROW IN YOUR WISDOM

Use what you already know
as a Base.
Open your mind to an open space.
Live and learn from all angle.
Life is not a simple sentence.
Explore with your big dream
Never think of a small team.
Love everyone freely.
Uplift and make it rain.
Blessings to the world,filled with
Awesome wisdom faces.
Grow in your wisdom.
Plant fruits in Paradise places.

SINGLE MOTHER

Single mother crying every night
Why are my burden so overbearing
Why does my struggles feel like a fight.
Why does my strength feels like a weakness.
Single mother feeling all alone
Why is my pain not yet gone.
Twisting and turning are the sheet from my bed
Why does my sweat feels like a flood.
Single mother rolls in the mud.
Gathering her thoughts into one love.
Fight to the end, you're alive and well.
Wake up from your dream and make up your bed.
Find your positive frame of mind. Use it to unwind.
Comfort your Soul into a peaceful Avenue.
Single mother I see you.
Because I was once a single mother too.

PEACEFUL MINDS

Relax and gather all your blessings.
Smile when you know your findings.
Show gratitude and use this as a new
beginning.
Pray for continuous guidance.
Meditate on deliverance.
Move Valleys, move Mountains.
Share with others will help to build
a peaceful mind.
You're never alone.
Peaceful
Peaceful
Minds.

YOU'RE MY VALENTINE

You make my knees buckle
You plug my ears with love
You send me beautiful Flowers
You Kiss my sorrows good bye.
You love me for me as you can see why.
You're my Valentine anniversary.
Everyday is a surprise sentiment.
My funny bone is weak.
My Heart always welcome you home.
I pinch your nose for a chuckle
I tickle your brain and wait for a whistle.
You're my Valentine, you make me this
comedy dress.
One more joke, and I will change into a
Princess clue.
You're my Valentines and I Love you.

FUTURE IN ME

You could see me as your bodyguard
Your moral support or your security.
Future in me is the Avenue clue.
You and I together just to name a few.
Love from the highest degree.
Rated by a higher power spree.
When you find the future in me.
Smile in this moment of distress
Bold is the energy used.
You could be my love stew.
Spicy with flavor and dew.
Unique is your future in me.
See you're a thinking machine
under the sheet..
I still hope you see a future with me
A very hard game to beat.
Now tickle my feet.

JAMAICAN SLANG

Pull in up mi selector
Rewind and come again.
This is a house filled with
jamming.
Pass mi the Rhythm from the
Reggae beat.
This is my time to feel sweet.
Rocking and enjoying the waves
Acting like uptown when I come
from the caves. Negril is my little
love shock, Rock it, It's my ball game
sock it. Soccer my Poem to a winning
machine seen.
Send me a unique degree.
A Jamaica Mi come from
Everything is almost free.
One Love from all my Legends.
Add me across the Board.
Versatile one, is my Jamaican slang.

PALM TREES

Hook me up with a tall Palm Tree.
Send him my Oak with a note inside
Palm Tree are the love of my life.
When is your time worth your while.
Fun is my joy to fame.
Nature is my passion game.
Accept or not, it's okay.
Palm Trees knows the sound of my
Heart beat, hurray.
Plant your love right here, Your growth
is my plant inside.
Explore and sway in the wind.
Palm Trees are my known expression.
In Love right away, with my Palm Tree.

PRACTICE A POSITIVE ATTITUDE

Adapt to a Positive attitude.
Success is your scope of practice.
Uplifting is your goal in mind
Use your skills to motivate others
in their crucial time.
You're never alone, be strong.
Spread the nature of love and shock
the world.
Practice a Positive attitude.
All the time.
Wear this as a motto, even if you're
from the Ghetto.
Live a positive life.

LET'S GET TOGETHER

What are you doing tonight
Let's get together.
What is your wildness imagination.
Set that on a roll call.
Think about your happy stream
then make a decision.
Let's get together when you find your
peace within.
Explore the universe then send me a
Grace ticket.
Mind you, this is your success too.
Let's get together and create a new
Avenue.
Set this in motion and lets dance
Read this poem and march along.
Togetherness is forever.
Build and grow together.
Like sisters and Brothers.
Let's get together.

FLOWERS LINES MY HEART

Deep in my Aorta
Deep between the Valves
Right between the heart beat
Flowers lines my Heart.
Send me flowers when I am
Happy, Send me flowers when I
am sad. On your way out.
Pick some Flowers for yourself.
Feel my energy through my smile
I can see your beautiful face.
When I die, lined my casket with
Flowers everywhere. Melt my heart
and send me to our supreme.
Waiting is his love to welcome me
home.
Peace is my thoughts, knowing that
Flowers lines my heart.

NOTHING IS WASTED

Nothing is wasted my friends
Everyone and everything pass
through your life for a reason.
Pack your baggage and wait to
face the next season.
Bend backwards for the one's in
need. Never forsake the homeless.
Feed everyone like a family tree.
Nothing is wasted when your left over
could be someone else bread.
Share with others and never waste a
thing. Break bread and welcome unity
To the end.

DO NOT SURRENDER IN HARD TIMES

Do not surrender in hard time
Instead hide until you accumulate
enough strength.
Fight through the difficult times
Embrace everything that comes along
with it.
Find an open space to breathe
Unwind with every new feelings.
Pray and ask for guidance.
In the end you will be strong enough to
help others.
Do not surrender in hard time.
Easy will be your forum next time around.
Enjoy new challenge around the bend.
Be brave, be a leader this time around.

I TRAVEL ALONE

I travel alone on earth
But deep within, I can
feel God's presense.
He whispered sweet poetry
to me in high demand and
high quality. My focus was always
to understand his call.
I travel alone for inspiration
I travel alone for a message
I travel alone to bond with the
higher Nature.
Yet I never feel alone at all...
My Heart is open to any question.
Should you wish to join me
You will not be travelling alone.
The path is already set for us to
Follow.
Yet by the bare eyes it seems like I
Travel alone.

ROAD TO SUCCESS

The road to Success is not easy.
Everything goes in the blink of an eye.
Use your passion to continue your dream
Seek and you will find success at the half
way mark.
Curve your knowledge and blend in with your
experiences. Practice will make near perfect
so look within.
Go get and redeem yourself.
Be bless, I am watching you. from the road
to success. Find true happiness along the way.
You're on the Road to Success.

I KISS MY CACTUS

I kiss my Cactus today.
ouch it never hurt for one minute.
Brave was my mind set.
Curious was my mood swing.
I kiss my Cactus today, this never
cost me a thing.
My eyes lights up and bounce off the
green. My knowledge plug in antioxidant .
I Kiss my Cactus today, In my dream
I would do this again.
Time for a Cactus juice, cheers to you.
Kiss a Cactus with me.
It is for free.

GOOD LIFE IS NOW

Good life is now
Better to know this than sorry
Best life will come when you
achieve your highest potential.
Reach for the Moon use it to
visit the Stars. Enjoy the Sun in
the same breath.
Be save in the moment.
Your Good life is now
Enjoy the Storms.
Use the Hurricane to over ride your
love for Nature. Rain is a blessing in
everything. Dance in the Rain and ask
for more green for your Garden.
Good life is now, your job is to enjoy it.
Reap what you sewed within the tree.
Your Goal is to love everyone, help to
build a good life now.

YOU'RE SPECIAL MY DEAR

You're Special my dear
Wear your special Dress
Wear your special attitude
to make a unique statement.
You're special my dear have
no fear.
Use you Heart to make a bond
Wrap it in a white handkerchief.
Open your hand then welcome
your poem. This is now a new
blessing.
You're special my dear
Your gift is in your hands.
Find positive energy from beyond
All Nation will join in.
Heal the sick and cure the poor
Find a way to make it work.
You're special my dear.
My gift to you, and mankind.

SUN ME TO DRY

Life without the Sun is like an
empty shell. Something missing
from within.
Sun me out to dry, give me some
Vitamin D. Stay away Sunburn.
No need for me to cry.
Lavish me with Nature Paradise.
Somewhere in the distance I can sense
a new Husband and for you a new Wife.
Smile, and add some Sunscreen on your
special child.
Sun me to dry just for a little while.
Whatever you do. Leave me off the line
to dry.

MY ADOPTED DOG MOLLY

Our furry friends are loyal.
Spending time with them
is crucial.
Focus on their health is vital
Fun time is everything and more.
No stress just jolly.
Close to my heart is my dog Molly.
You can relate, I saw your little princess
running through your gate.
Waggling her furry tail, excited to see you
home.
Now you can relate, I can just imagine your
Pit bull taking you down. Wrestling and counting
to three. Fun time for you to see.
Adopt a furry friend today. Be a funny Bunny.
I just love my dog Molly.
I have to go she's calling me.

A HUSBAND WILL FIND YOU

Adjust to society,find your circle
Focus on the strength in you.
Social to a limit, afford events
with no tickets. Free first just to
scope. Remember men don't walk
with a note. Feel out your goal in mind.
Always be very kind.
Forget about any doubt sickness
Everyone is looking your way.
Your Awesome and amazing,
This is true. Someday your
Husband will find you.
To show balance, I cannot be partial
This is life, someday you will find
yourself a wife. Look around,
she's right over there.
Cheers.

AROUND THE BEND

Around the bend is your success
Why are you stopping here.
Keep your eyes on the wall green.
Send your Hope our there.
Around the bend is your future
Why your Focus ends with today.
Jump in your success suit.
Send me a spare.
Around the bend you will find
new underwear. Smile for this
poem is your new career boost.
Work it girl walk the run way.
Send me a thank you for I am
still around the bend.
Scraping what is left from success.
Yes! you're the best.

SON KNOWS BEST

My son is my God given gift
I Love him more everyday.
He's my everything
He's my every holiday prayer.
His smiles open my heart.
His genuine soul is mine to keep.
His unique self is from my Dna
He knows my energy so well.
This is no test.
My son knows me best.
Our hearts beats as one.

DAUGHTER'S NEED THEIR DADS

Where is daddy to help me out
Where is daddy to pick up the pieces
Where is daddy in difficult times.
Why do I need strangers to see me unwind.
Where is daddy when I need a hug.
Where is daddy when I was lied to about love.
Where is my daddy to bail me out.
I feel so innocent in this world of the unknown.
Where is daddy to throw me a crown.
Not trying to introduce whining or fabrication.
All daughters needs their daddy love in one motion.
To guide them through difficult times.
Daughters first learn to trust one man.
Daddy Love.

LOVE ALL YOUR CHILDREN

Fathers love all your children
Mothers love all your children.
Even the one's who came into
this world wearing a cheating spouse
jacket, some children feel like bastards too.
Hurtful as it sounds they're your babies.
Show them the rope of your true love.
Bond with them until the end.
The child that was born blind folded
Feeling their way around on the survival
scale, will be the only child standing on
your gray day. Trying to help on your mayday.
So you try to apologize, but you don't know
where to start. So much unanswered questions
yet not much time.The only child standing is
your only child left.
My advice to you, learn to love all your children.
In every circumstances.

STAY THROUGH STRUGGLES

Stay through struggles
Abide with me and stay still.
Do not run away in difficult times.
Instead let's hold hands for a
connection stride.
Give me some heat to warm things up.
Send me some water to fill my cup.
I will give you a shelter so you can
think straight. We're not alone under
this struggles gate.
Focus on what matters.
Faith, Family and Friends.
Stay together and struggle no more.
Learn to build think positive door.

TRUMP FEVER

Trump Fever Is beyond the norm.
That is the first sign of an infection.
Reduce the Heat with some water.
Maybe one candidate will bark like a dog
to set things straight and in order.
So much madness going on with Trump fever
Not even sure if it's from America.
This is not a cold. It's more than a concussion.
Low blows and plain knock out.
Trump winning with knowing very little about
Politics. Trump Fever will be that effective.
Ask no question just Vote with your eyes closed.
Trump Fever will give you a drive home.
In that free white Limousine.
Funny driver from JAmerica.
Everyone will be affected by this Trump Fever.
Apply your open mind to history forever.

MY HEAVENLY FATHER OWNS THE WORLD.

I never feel less than
Even if you feel like I should.
I never feel loss
Even though I could.
When I think of my journey
I see where I could help others
to over come challenges.
My first feeling is why worry
When I know for a fact that my
heavenly Father owns the world.
Spring out and make waves
This is everyone play date.
No more feeling shame or disgrace.
His love goes along way.
Come on let's pray.
Our Father owns the world.
This is a daily prayer to uplift each other.
As sisters and brothers.

SAFETY FIRST.

Safety first
Stay Focus
Safety first is
Always your
Blanket.
Seek and you
will find.
Everything
Necessary to
Sustain life.
Remember
Safety first.
In all cause.
Look, Listen
and feel is a
Start.

Equipped with
a code card.
Check all drawers.
Code Red
Code Blue
Code Amber.
Just to name a
few.
Safety first.
You will know
What to do.
Help others first
in Safety first.
That's the EMT
in me.

STOP THE VIOLENCE

Stop the violence in your neighborhood
Be a Mentor.
Help the youths with their learning experience
Teach them about growth and pain.
Stop the violence, make a statement
Help others gain a wanted experience.
Be the bigger brother
Be a bigger Sister.
Love across the board.
When you try to Stop the Violence.
You could be the next President.

JAMAICAN PATOIS

Pull it up mi selector
Rewind and come again.
Let's start over, go and
tell your friends.
That Jamaican Patois
from way yonder is in the
Area.
What a gwaan means how
you doing.
Relax yuh mind and feel
cooling.
Jamaican Patois in America
Surviving on every corner.
One Love culture is the
Jamaican Patois.
Big up all Jamaicans.
Nuff Respect every time.
A Jamaica mi come from man.
Yuh gallang.
Wid yuh bad self.

COVER MY BRAIN

Cover my Brain
Too much information
I don't want to go insane.
Shelter me from gossip and
Negative Vibes.
Too much of your Pain.
Seek an Avenue to renew
your mind. Keep active all
the time. Less about others
focus on what makes you a
better person. Too Vain
Please cover my Brain.
Smile you're a unique soul.
Start with a festive mood.
Borrow my cool shoes
Dance to the mellow mood
Now cover my Brain .
I Don't want to cast no blame.
You already know my name.
Poetry Flame coming from my
membrane.
So Cover my Brain.

SMILE ONE MORE TIME.

Smile, one more time
I just want to see your smile again.
Drop the energy that eats away your
personality my friend.
Stop! and pick up some memorable
moments. Do you remember our
love poems days.
Come over read it to me again
Try, just one more time my friend.
I want to see your sparkling smile again.
No more dull moment.
Yes we're on the same road again
Searching deep in the Wilderness for
our smile to blend in.
This is not the end, It's the beginning of
a renewed friendship.
Smile.

EXTRAORDINARY 0400AM.

Wake up my beautiful Angel.
This is your moment in time
Write until you're out of words.
This is a unique gift.
From a unique Soul.
Write at 0400AM
This is your Mandatory Poem
Every Morning at 0400Am.
I am with your thoughts
Pray then Meditation.
After that you can move Mountains.
Beyond the skies are your Dreams
Sending directly from me.
Sleep my beautiful Angel.
Chosen Poet is you.
Extraordinary one.

WE WILL FACE DISASTER

We will face disaster
Sometime in life.
This sounds scary
But you should have a
Disaster Plan.
Safety first is our every
move. Make Jesus our
Best guide for sure.
We will face disaster
I will face disaster blues
In all challenges we
should know what to do.
Help others along the way.
Faith, Food and Shelter.
Love will carry everyone
Through the danger.
We will face Disaster together
Be my Shoulder, and I will be
your Rock.

UPLIFT EACH OTHER

Uplift each other in times of need
Find a path to accommodate others
Never try to go it alone.
Bond like sisters and brothers
Uplift in time of Trials, never try to do
it alone. Find peace within your soul.
Forgive in temptation bound.
Breathe deep within the storm
I am with you always.
This should be the norm.
Uplift each other Careers.
Far far away in the Air.
Creative one is always near.

POETRY MACHINE

Poetry Machine plug me in
Send me a life line to sweep
away my sins.
Play my favorite Poem
Put me in the mood.
Save my moments to enjoy
this green food.
Poetry Machine everyone
Toy. It's created to bring us joy.
Eat from my plate ask security
to open the gate.
Poetry Machine is mine to keep
Forever you will remember my feet.
Next time this will be a retreat.

GENIUS IDEAS

Blow my mind with a Genius idea.
Never seen or heard before.
Close your eyes and see me in the
mirror. Create your unique idea.
Incorporate the Nation flavor.
Fill in Nature in the blank spaces
Find room to be original bases.
Poetry is a work of Art, a Genius Idea.
Now show me your chart.
Make waves not too far apart.
Wow, what a Genius idea.

COME AND BREAK BREAD WITH ME

Come and break bread with me.
Sit down under this Mango Tree.
No need to worry about a thing
When God made me, he gave me
wings.
Come and break bread with me my dear
Someday we will own a Fair.
Gathering little children with their Parents
to have a good time.
Adults only can have a glass of red wine.
Come and break bread with me.
It's always free. Bread for everyone on your
family Tree. Compliments from my Poetry.

YOU'RE AN ANGEL

Deep in my Dream
Deep in my deep deep sleep
I can see the eyes of an Angel.
Not much explaining to do.
You were wearing my favorite shoe
Never in the history of mankind
This is not humanly possible.
When I open my eyes .
I could see clearly that you were
that Angel.
Always by my side. In the most
Crucial times.
You were my Guardian Angel
I think of you all the time.
Deep,deep in my sleep.

I CAN'T SEE YOUR FACE.

Move the blanket from your eyes
I cannot see your face.
Be the one to be my guide in this
world filled with disgrace.
Open your heart and let go of stress
Everyone has some form of problem.
Move the Curtain away from your eyes
You're a beautiful emblem.
Safety is your first impression
Believe in yourself.
Move the guilt from your face
You're not the only one in this place.
Forgiveness will be yours to accept
Move on and motivate at your best.
Now I can really see your face.
Awesome one.
Spread your love today.
In every possible way.

WHY ARE YOU CRYING

Tear Drops, tear drops
This is a holiday
Why are you crying on
this festive day.
Can we enjoy without
thinking about the ones
we lost.
They wants us to remember
the good times at no cost.
Move on in every circle with
a goal in mind.
Be happy for awhile.
Instead of crying all the time.
Focus on me, I will be your
support happy blanket for free.

I MOVED ON

I moved on from all the pain you
cost me.
I release them in the Air for free.
I moved on from the shame you
brought me.
I sink them in the ocean deep into
the sea.
I moved on from all the Negativity
I now live with my Positive one
I moved on, so now I am bless to
write this poem.
You can turn it into a song.
I moved on from destruction.

TAKE A PEEK

Take a peek at my idea
Give me a piece of your
Cake.
Blend both to make a new
Avenue, someday we will relate.
Take a Peek of the future now
Yet today is still at stake
Enjoy my unique expression
Everyone has a birthday faith.
Take a Peek of yesterday
This is now your birthday.
Cake.
Surprise anniversary.
Take a peek.

TAKE ME ON A CRUISE

Take me on a Cruise my love
Kiss me forever more.
Never let me loose
Capture my soul to
blend with yours.
Take me on a Cruise
I just want to get away.
Free to explore the views.
Shower me to relax only with
you. The one with my Trust
for Avenue.
Take me on a Cruise.
I do love you.
Let's enjoy the shows.
For another clue.
Mellow mood.
Exotic foods.
Everything on a Cruise.

MERCY AT YOUR DOOR

Mercy is at your door
Open and let him in.
He has forgiven you of
your sins.
Forgiveness is shared
among us. Pass it around.
Enjoy and move on.
Mercy is at your door
Open and let him in.
Have Mercy on all.
Forgive and forget.
Answer your call.
Rise again from your fall.

LOVE ME OPENLY

Love me openly
Feel free, my heart is yours.
Love me Openly do not close
the inner doors.
Keep your eyes on my loyalty
My eyes can see your face.
Love me openly for who I am
Expect the same truth from my
space.
Open my heart, I already unlock
yours
Loving you openly is easy.
One mind body and Soul.
That's all my scope can see.
One Unit with you.

I WILL TRAVEL THE WORLD

I will travel the world
until I find happiness.
I will slow down just so
we can play catch up.
I will send my hope and
dreams wrap in a blanket
Just for Mr Right to view.
Then caption it.
I will Travel the world and
enjoy every given person
Our uniqueness will shock in
place our Diversity.
I will travel the world with you.
True happiness begins with
suspense.
Use it for a head rest.
Then test, the best.

MAKE A ROOF

Hello Sir
Make a Roof over the Desert
Invite the Nation to a Humanity
Challenge.
Give each person Hope and
Persuverance to work with.
Use the Sun for light.
Safety is yours to distribute.
Find true love deep within.
Poetry is the moment you're
not sure exactly what I am speaking
about. So put me to work too.
Madam I see and feel your pain
Pray for guidance.
Our creator already know how to find
us.

JAMAICA IRIE MAN

Jamaica Irie man
You should take a
Vacation.
Enjoy the food and
Travels and Reggae band
Enjoy the people with a
patois slang.
Out of many we're one
Jamaica Irie man.
Put on your best Sunday
dress. Go sing on the
Choir and be bless.
Jamaica Irie man.
Every one have a plan.
Welcome every woman
Find peace within.
No one is an Island
And no man will stand alone.
Jamaica Irie man.
Roots Rock and Reggae
Yes! Jamaica Irie man.

BE YOUR OWN ADVOCATE

Be your own Advocate
Represent yourself.
Uplift others, but always
remember to uplift you too..
Be your own advocate.
Set the stage, know your
potential page.
Always believe in yourself.
Reach for the highest mountain
Be one step of the mind game.
Never focus on the one that will
stop you in your track.
Be your own advocate.
You're stronger than they think.
Win from a different angle.
Promote yourself too.
True advocate is you.

SPREAD YOUR WINGS

Spread your wings
You're a leader
Why do you want to
settle as a follower.
Spread your wings
on twitter.
Make a note that you're
no quitter.
While you spread your wings
Search for goal finders and
successful builders.
Explore Nature with the Sunrise in
view. Embrace and welcome all.
Spread your wings, help others
while you enjoy every call.
Be creative in your adventures.
Spread your wings and fly.
Far,far away.

ALWAYS SAY HALLELUJAH

I walk for a moment then I give praises.
I talk in disbelieve to myself,so I still give
praises. Hallelujah,Hallelujah.
You lost your job through hatred,give praises.
You got sick,you never saw this coming
You got divorce,now you're getting Married
Give praises. Hallelujah,Hallelujah,Hallelujah.
We're family with different situation.
We're family with different challenges
We're family with different circumstances
We're family with different blessings
In everything let's give praises.
Hallelujah,Hallelujah,Hallelujah,Hallelujah.
Praise his Holy name.

FREE TO PASS JUDGEMENT

Welcome criticism with open arms
Everyone is free to pass judgement
This energy won't cost a thing.
So it's waste of time to invest in passing
judgement.
Let it pass you by the wayside.
Welcome an open Panel
Everyone need a Forum
To express one self.
Plug in your Wisdom
Then comprehend.
Everyone is free to cost Judgement
The sky is not the limit.
So judge not.
Now it's Free to pass me by the way side
Because I won't judge you.
Yet it's free to pass Judgement.
But would you.

SPANISH NEEDLE A CURE

Spanish Needle, a Flower that runs
wild. Backyards are filled with them
But very few people knows this Miracle.
In my Culture it's like a man best friend.
PSA is off base,well let's drink some then.
Spanish Needle. Remember Jamaicans
speak Patois not spanish.
This Bush is very powerful, I would recommend
for all American President for testing.
Spanish Needle knows no Border and It will not
build walls. An open book to compliment
Diversity. Spanish Needle, what if our Ancestors
recommend this Bush to cure Cancer.
What would be your question for your doctor.
A dream holding on to the Spanish Needle cure.
Open mind Gallery,for sure.
Spanish Needle.
Como se llama.
Bidens Pilosa.

NATION POET

Jamaica, America two
very challenging countries.
My Roots is mixed with my
Faith and family.
My greatest gift in America
was the birth of my Son Edgar.
Both Countries sharing my
Legacy. Poetry is everything
and more. I love people so
Someday I will write for the Nation.
Nation Poet with an Jamaican Accent.
A son with an American Accent.
Jamerican Poet to spread across
the Nation.
Help yourself and don't be no brag.

GOSSIP ROOM

Why do I need to hear what
you heard about me.
Why do I Need to tell you what
was said about you.
This energy gossip causes too
much conflict.
Remove yourself from the Gossip
Room, too much hurt within the schools.
Believe in yourself and Focus on that
Let hear say take a back seat gal.
No need for gossip to be promoted
A lot more jobs in the Sea.
Swim until you reach the top.
Gossip people are drowning.
I can only call for help, because I can't
swim. Gossip will eat away your mayday.
Stay within your circle,love everyone at
the same level.
No need for the Gossip Room.
Why are you leaving so soon madam.

STEP IN A STYLE

Step out inna style
Step out inna Rhythm
Capture the hearts and
uplift your culture.
Remember your sisters and
your brothers.
Step out inna Reggae
Step out Inna Faith
Everyone is a winner
Right here in this place.
Come on man
Come on mi lady
Step out inna Rhythm
Step out inna Style
This is strictly Patois Style.
Every time.
We Stepping out.

MARKETING BOOSTER

This is your product on the market
My two hands are up.
Can you see your product now
This is not a teaser .
Allow me to be your Marketing Booster.
Products must go now.
Order the best in the business.
You have the number one product
Focus and market that.
Positive mind works all the time.
Remember hand out some freebies
first. Music and a Selector.
Come again. Pull it up mi selector
Rewind and come again.
Re-introduce your Marketing Booster.
Cheap+Best =Your Order.
Nuff Respect to the marketing Booster
line.
Every time.

JUMP OUT OF THE GATE

Jump out of the gate
Start your life over
Success is at your door.
Open and let it in.
Jump out of the gate
You're locked up for too
long.
This is a Free world.
Everyone will learn to get
a piece of success.
Come here my dear
Life is not fear.
Hold the handle and steer
it your way.
You're a gifted soul
Let's plug in your latest
Project.
Jump out of the gate
Be bold,be Brave.
Go get it.

TREES AS THE ROOT

Someday in the middle of nowhere
I will be the distant shadow,
Waiting to see your demeanor.
Someday in the distance I will still carry a smile,
Nothing or no one can take it away.
Someday in the wilderness I will build a house,
So no one will be lost no more.
Someday, someday, someone will build a roof over the desert
instead of building a wall.
Shelter for travelers who's passion is Nature.
Someday, someday I will build a Poetry bed to relax my head.
Free for all sleep.

EVERYDAY IS A HOLIDAY

Everyday is a holiday
Celebrate in every moment.
Enter your mindset with your favorite music.
Apply your favorite poem to marinade things.
Dress to impress yourself
Smile in every moment
Enjoy yourself and don't leave room for stress
Everyday is a vacation too
Carry on your success to represent you
Stand straight in a glass house
Cheers to a vacation well spent.

SUNSHINE PEEPS FOR FUN

I woke up to nature banging
Thunder and lightning standing at my front door
With my eyes barely open
I still was able to say,
Thank you Jesus for the blessings
Wind then sends the trees swaying
Raindrops draw me outside to write this poem
Apply my creativity for the finishing
Glossy finish just for you my friends
It pays to be me
Nature will find room in my heart everytime for free
Mankind can judge with one goal in mind
Soccer is my roots
New growth everyday
Nature paradise will swept us away
Sunshine peeps for fun

BE MY VALENTINE

Be my valentine
Be the one I come home to
Be the one I love to share my most intimate moments with
Be that shoulder to cry on
That rock to embrace with a touch of love to marinade through it
Be a foundation that will never crumble easy
Stand in the wilderness and able to survive the storm
Be my love
My rock
My foundation
Survive life challenges together
A poetry recipe for my tea
This one is free
Happy valentines with love
For real

SMILE AND LIVE

In every corner you will find happiness
In every corner you will find challenges
In every corner you will find perseverance
In every corner you will find someone to fit every situation
Uplift yourself out of the corner
Then make it your own
A box won't work so turn it new
Then be your best with your GPS
Explore your mind, fun to be creative
Smile and live

STOP MY POEMS ARE TALKING

When the root gets enough water
The energy looks brighter
When the sunlight flashes
The branches laugh at loud
When your love travels
Then the leaves travels too
Smile at this point
Because the root of this tree is you

LIFE IS A GOOD EDUCATION

Make the best out of life
Even if it throws you lemons
Uplift yourself
Then walk out with oranges
Life is like a fruit
It's enjoyed by everyone
Sometimes, distractions interferes with good intentions
Embrace then motivate one on one
Life is a mountain filled with sand
Count with a goal in mind
Life is a good education

My american son Edgar, my adopted dog Molly, both
shared my heart. Faith, Family, and Friends, my motto.